TRUMP! ON THE RUN

TREMENDOUSLY WRITED AND DRAWINGED SO BEST BY BRANDON MORINO

BMA

2020 is FAKE NEWS

Trumpy On The Run
Copyright © 2020 Brandon Morino

ISBN-13: 978-0-9969950-4-7

Written by Brandon Morino

Illustrated by Brandon Morino

Approved by Trumpy
(he thought it was a color-by-numbers book)

Nothing has gone right for Trumpy since "Trumpy Unleashed". In fact, it's the opposite!

Once atop the Maralago Adult Center world as the self-proclaimed King of Everything, two scandals have sent him on the lam from the law. Fleeing (it appears) from prosecution, a "Coalition Of The Willing" sets off after him, employing as many tactics and gadgets as possible to nab Sir Cheeto and bring him back to the insane asylum where he belongs.

Along the way, Trumpy and his companions will run across state lines, socio-economic stratas, zealots from both ideological extremes, no fewer than 60 MFC locations, 550 cheeseburgers, pedophioles, prostitutes, furry Nazis, psycho actors, and Bernie Lovers. But with the strength of his "friends" (a hand puppet and a scheming sub sandwich), he's determined to run the gauntlet and make it to the promised land.

So sit back, flip on FoxNews or MSNBC, unbag your cheesburger, unzip your pants, chug your soda, get your Twitter fingers warmed up, ignore the facts, and enjoy Trumpy On The Run.

Brandon Morino

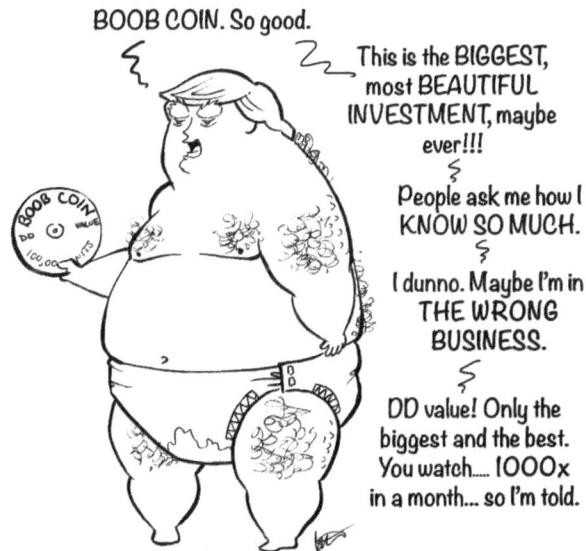

BOOB COIN. So good.

This is the BIGGEST, most BEAUTIFUL INVESTMENT, maybe ever!!!

People ask me how I KNOW SO MUCH.

I dunno. Maybe I'm in THE WRONG BUSINESS.

DD value! Only the biggest and the best. You watch..... 1000x in a month... so I'm told.

They'll NEVER catch me, 'cause I'm so fast. I'm TERRIFICALLY fast. I'm so fast, I'm FASTER than fast. People ask me, "How are you SO FAST?" I know these things, OKAY?!

....aaannnd a leaking, hopping sandwich is beating you. But, if FoxNews says so...

HOP-A-LONG CRUSTITY

THE TRUTH IS OUT THERE

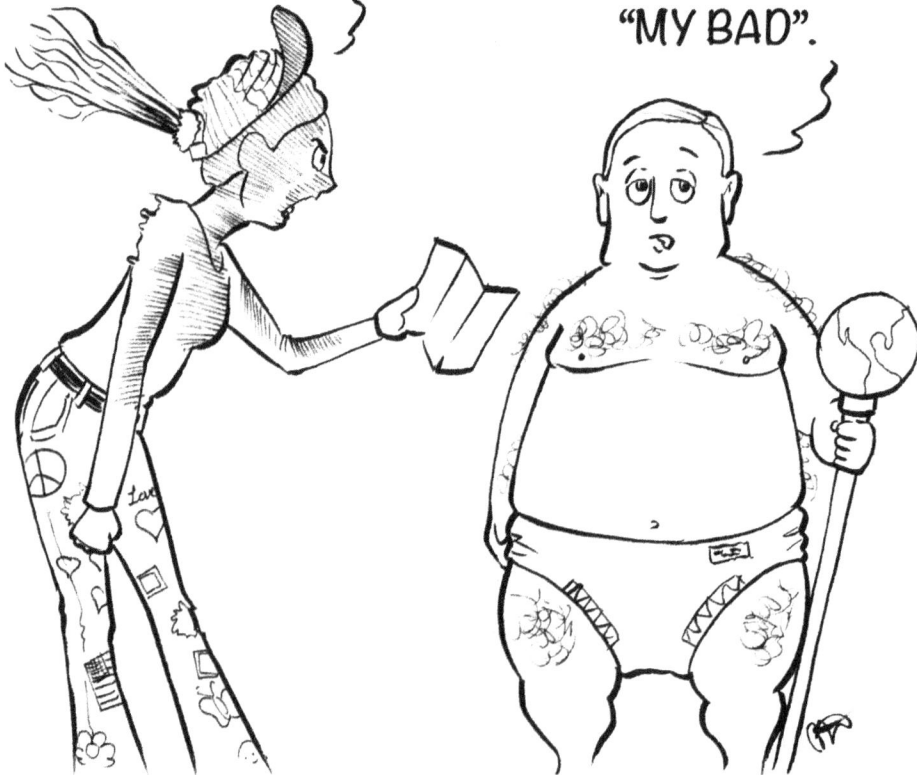

POPULAR HALLMARK "GAG CARD" IN RUSSIA

So, you're saying that you've got a video of Trumpy doing something disgusting? More disgusting than how he already is? And THIS is why he ran away? Sorry, but I can IMAGINE Trumpy doing some incredibly disgusting things.

....and there's also a pink bunny and floating fart head listening in on this conversation? You're not shocking me, Pooty.

But, video is, how you say... "Moist and creamy!"

DA!

THE POINT OF NO RETURN

7

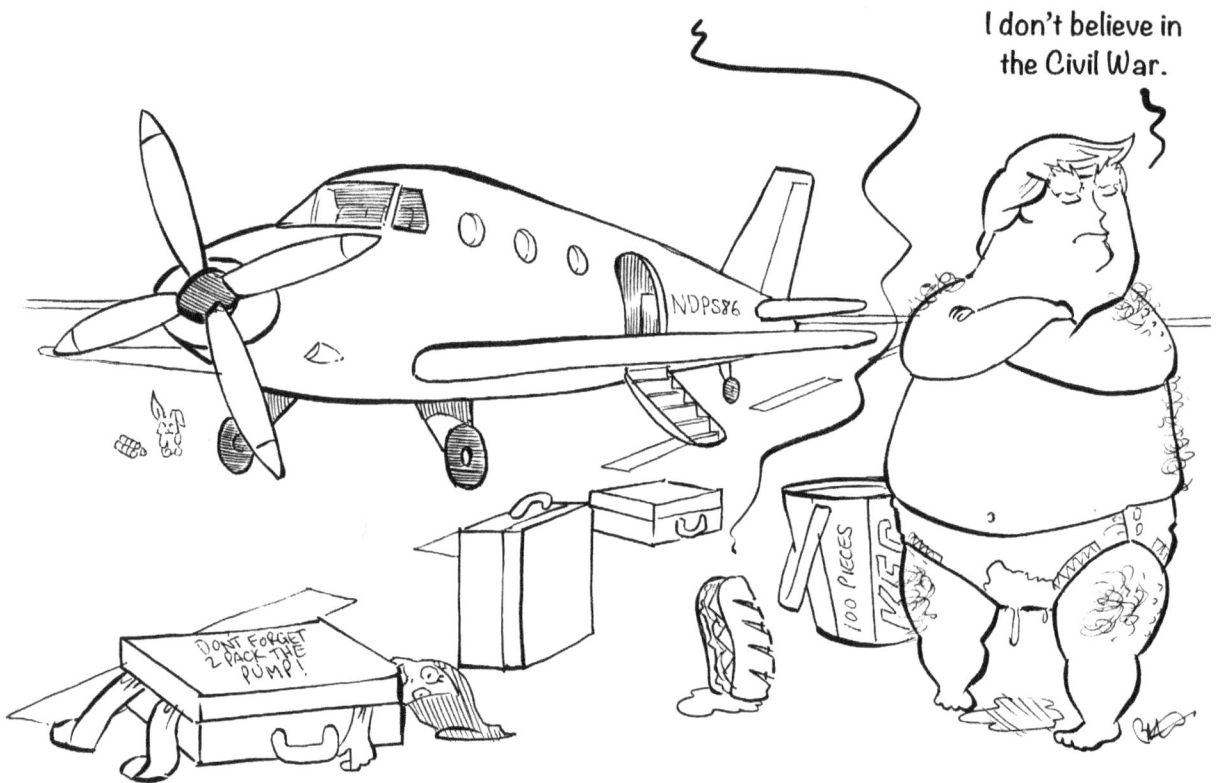

PLANES FROM THE CIVIL WAR ARE SOOOOO 19TH CENTURY

For the FIFTH TIME: a mullet wearing, Coors Light chuging, YUGE MOSQUITO is not uncommon in FLORIDA. My gawd, you LIVE there. Thought you'd know this by now.

Drone!!! DRONE!! Deep state!! Liberal FBI!!!

BECAUSE FLOR-I-DUHHHH

POWER LINES DOUBLE AS HANDY RECHARGERS

METHOD TO THE MADNESS

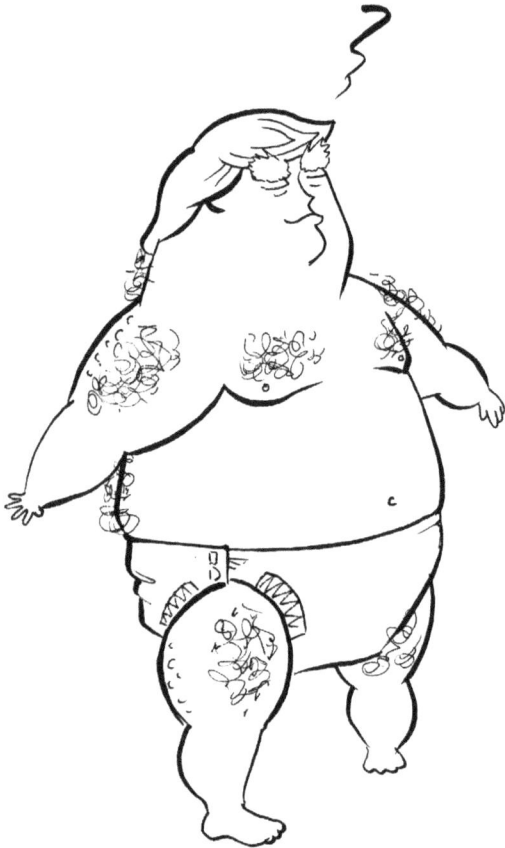

ALSO DOUBLES AS MAYO FOR CHEESEBURGERS

EASY MONEY! WHAT COULD GO WRONG?

FROM THE PAN TO THE FLAMES

CROSSING OF ARMS IS CODE FOR "HELP ME!"

IGNORANCE IS BLISS

A SUE-HAPPY, HYPERSEXUAL, MEGALOMANIACAL, NARCISSISTIC, imaginarily wealthy but BROKE-AS-HELL, PREDATORIAL music producer. We shoulda known!!

Ow! You broke my BACK!!! I'm gonna sue you!!!!

Well, the "music producer" part is new, so...

"DRIPPING" WITH IRONY

LOST IN TRANSLATION

THERE'S NO LOGIC IN RELIGION

"DRIPPING" WITH IRONY, PART TWO

DAD JOKES, THE REVENGE

OVERT RACISM VS COVERT RACISM

You can't defeat me!!! I've REPLAC'D you with a QUIZN'Z ROBOT SUB programm'd ta destroy him, being as he destroy'd ME. Mah plan is werkin' perfectly! On a personal note, ah can't believe I FIGUR'D OUT where yer mouth was on the FIRST TRY.

LUCKY YOU! TIME TA BUY A LOTT'RY TIKUT.

NOT EVERYTHING TASTES LIKE CHICKEN

BECAUSE ROBOTS DON'T "GET" NUANCE

NOTHING TO SEE HERE

WHAT A GREAT IDEA(S)!!!

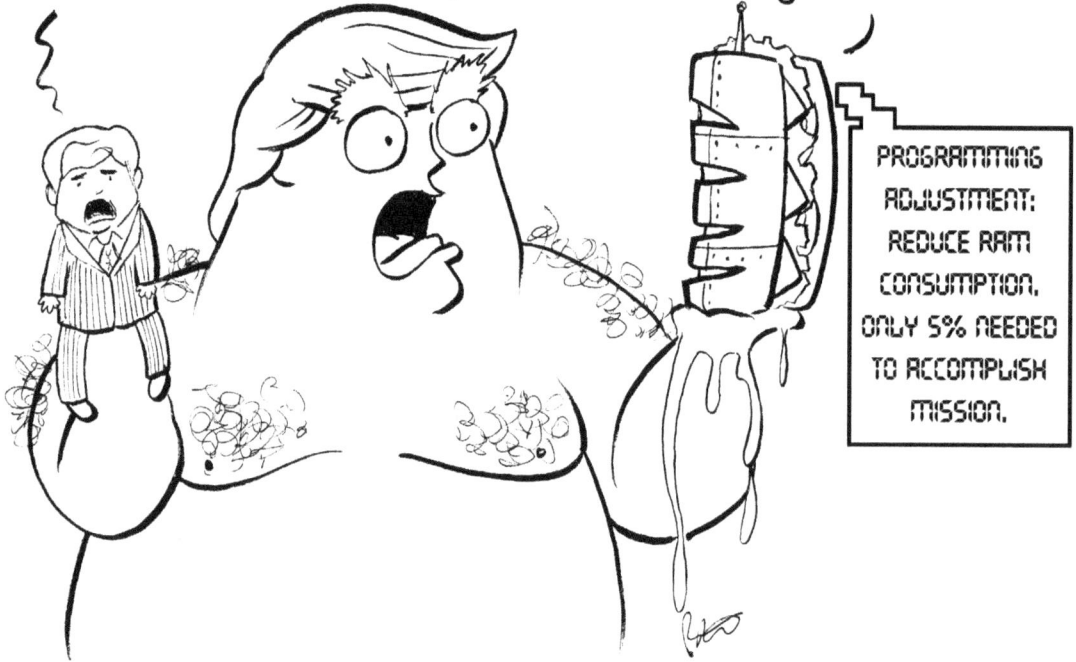

QUANTUM SOLUTION TO A 64K PROBLEM

INTELLIGENCE IS NO MATCH FOR STRONG AND STICKY

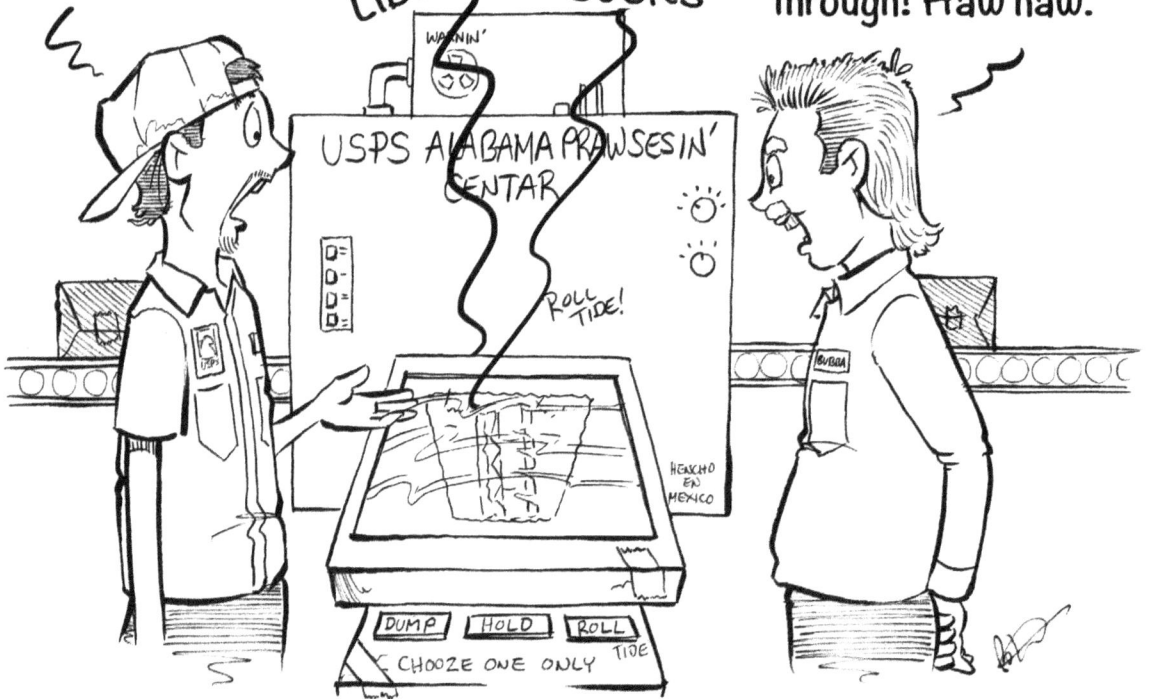

THAT'S HOW WE DO IT IN THE SOUTH

ONE BOMB REPLACED WITH ANOTHER

NEXT UP: PAROLE SEX

Of COURSE he did it. Has nahwledge that is GREAT, I do. Titties!! Helps you, me cans. Hmmmmmm! Nuthing rong! Pleed the 5th!! Can I has TITTIES?!! Pookie gurls!!!

It's like an over-caffinated Yoda, with TORRETS.

Why does he look so familiar?

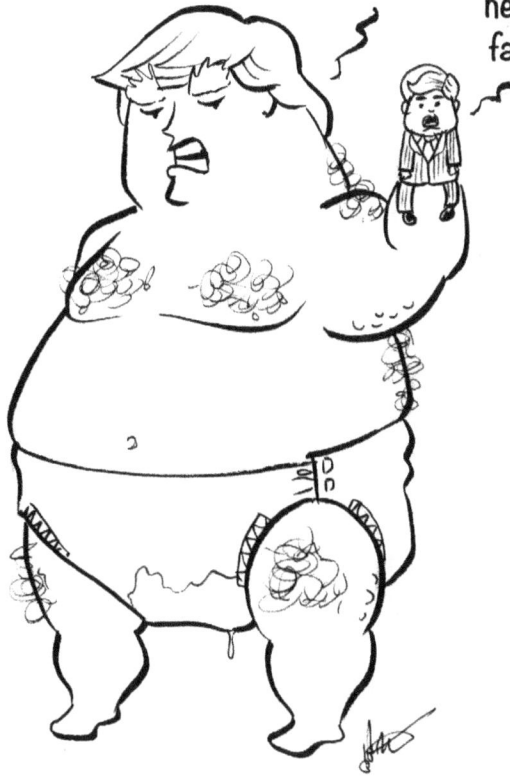

A CREATURE UNCLASSIFIED IN NATURE

WOW!! That was one TOTALLY disturbed dude. I mean, did you HEAR him? Conspiracy thoeries, revisionist history, fake news, Sharpies that can move hurricanes, diets that kill, miracle cures, hookers... he was ALL OVER THE PLACE.

Wow! These are GREAT talking points.. what was that THIRD one again?

HAS A FAMILIAR RING TO IT

GIRLS GONE WILD, THE FINALE

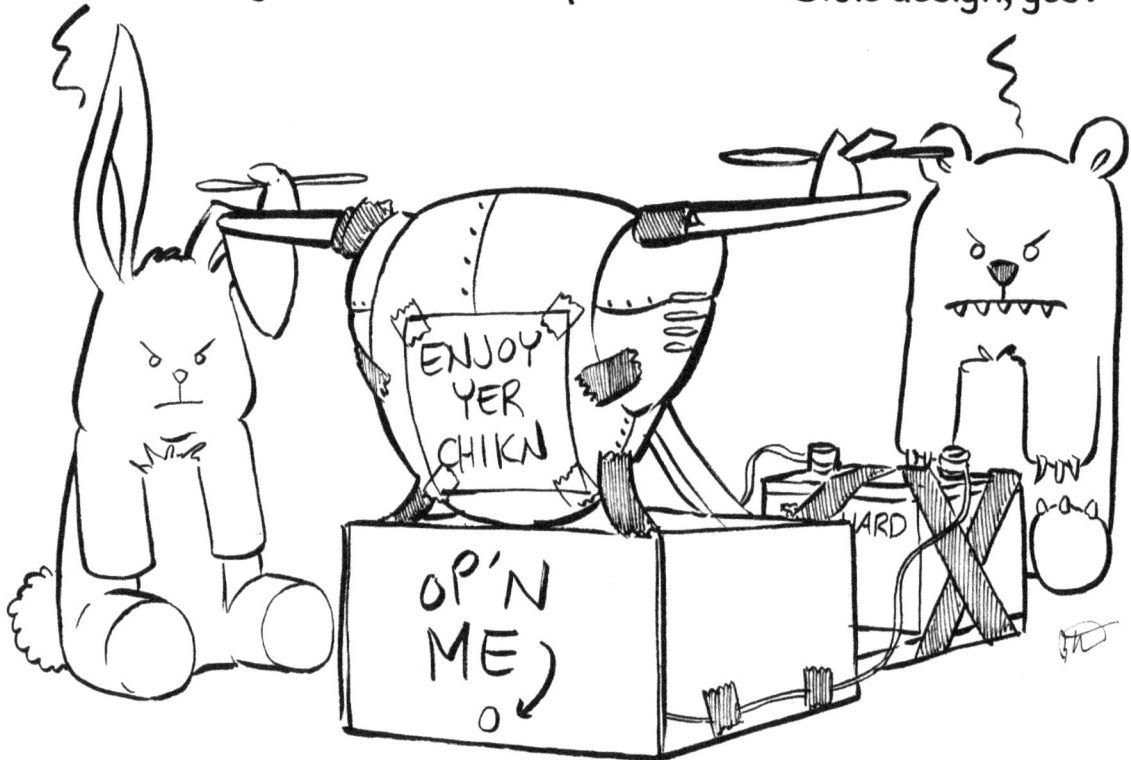

SOUTHERN INGENUITY MEETS SOVIET BUILD QUALITY

A CUT SCENE FROM LORD OF THE RINGS

Wow! That was weird. He just lit on fire like a PROGRESSIVE winning the lottery, not wanting to give it all away, and realizing they have become part of the ONE PERCENT.

The smell of that burning New York Goombah Grease is making me hungry.

Pre...cious..

BZZT   BZZT

AS LIT AS MARRYING YOUR COUSIN

DUMB IS LACK OF EDUCATION, WHICH MEANS YOU CAN'T
READ THE RESEARCH, WHICH MEANS INABILITY TO
UNDERSTAND SCIENCE... OR ANYTHING ELSE.

This disguise is so TOTALLY TERRIFIC.
Liberals HATE their own kind. They'll
SOOOOOO stay away from us.

Liberals would EAT
their own, too.. if they
weren't all VEGAN.
I heard THAT on
FoxNews.

LOOK! Alec
Baldwin's gone
DOUBLE
METHOD

He's so
BRAVE!

BRAVE LIKE A SUBURBAN WHITE HOUSEWIFE

BIRDS DON'T UNDERSTAND GENTRIFICATION

THE ULTIMATE KRYPTONITE

BYRON'S ABOUT TO LOSE IT

LIKE TRUMPY IS A HUMAN... BARELY

ANOREXIC, ZERO IQ, FAKE BLONDE "CHILDREN OF THE CORN"
CRAZY-EYED FOXNEWS WOMEN ARE THE PERFECT MEDICINE

THE POWDER IS SOFT AND WHITE, GREAT FOR
CARVING STRAIGHT LINES

Billionaires are losing rape cases nationwide, the stock market is teetering on the brink of collapse, glorious generational WHITE WEALTH is vanishing before our very eyes, and viewers are fleeing FoxNews!! These are REAL problems

All YOU care about is a stupid insect, you SANTA FE FREAK.

PETA ♡

SAVE THE SOUTHWESTERN WILLOW FLYCATCHER

SAVE THE ENDANGERED WHITEOUS PRIVILEDGIOUS GOP MOSQUITO FROM EXTINC... NO, WAIT...

TONEE O, QUICK WITH THE PUNS

Sorry. The Boris Johnson style ended with BREXIT and the Owen Wilson style ended 20 years befor... sorry, TEN years before that. I forgot "Little Fockers". That was mildly amusing.

TOO FAT TO SURF, SO NO THIRD OPTION

There's some oily, SWAMP-LIKE muck that's built up over time. Gonna have to clean it up before I can fix the root of the matter.

JUST LIKE THE AMAZON

Not a horrible Conserative Christian Opinion News Pundit hairstyle. It makes me wanna lie to a camera and pimp elderly-focused products.

I asked for the Charlottesville. I'm conflicted about it.

POMPOUS PUNDIT AND PROUD BOY: THE SERIES

DRAWING THE LINE WITH A SHARPIE

It's a GOOD THING they sell the Vintage Trent Lott "Glory Years" Edition. I feel complete again... you, however, so totally UNFAIR.

Who's BOB MARLEY? Was he a hippie? As long as he was WHITE..

VOTED SANTA FE'S BEST

Dianna's WIGS
AND BEAUTY SUPPLIES

DON'T GO CRAZY ABOUT YOUR HEAD, COVER IT UP WITH A WIG.

Cover up your DEFECTS

CLOSE ENOUGH

PLACED ON HOLD WHILE THEY GET THE MANAGER

ANYBODY WHO SAYS "HUH?" NEEDS TO GET A LIFE

I'm SOOO the BEST costume on Halloween... almost, but probably the BEST. So I'm told by SOOOO many people. So many, I can't even explain. You'd be shocked.

They're not telling you to be a PEACH. What's WRONG with you?!!!!

100% GEORGIA PEACH

LOST IN TRANSLATION... AGAIN

Peach Cobbler? I love peach... PEACH??
Impeach??? NO! Get it AWAY from me!!

IPTSD (IMPEACH TRUMPY STRESS DISORDER)

THE INEVITABILITY OF LIFE

BEGGARS CAN'T BE CHOOSERS

THE COMFORT COWBOY IS THE HERO WE DESERVE

THE TRUTH IS OUT THERE

BONE APE A TEET

ROLLING IN DOUGH

These feel GREAT!! Money well spent. Feels good to be a closet-case LIMO LIBERAL again.

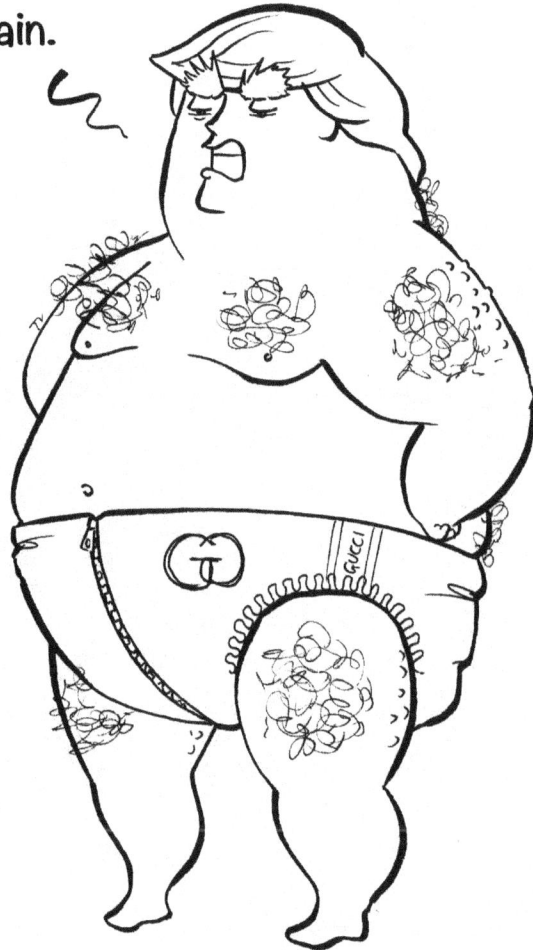

We really coulda used that money for... WAIT!!... You were WHAT, again??? MY RIGHT WING LIFE IS A LIE!!!

LATE TO THE GAME IS BETTER THAN NOT SHOWING UP

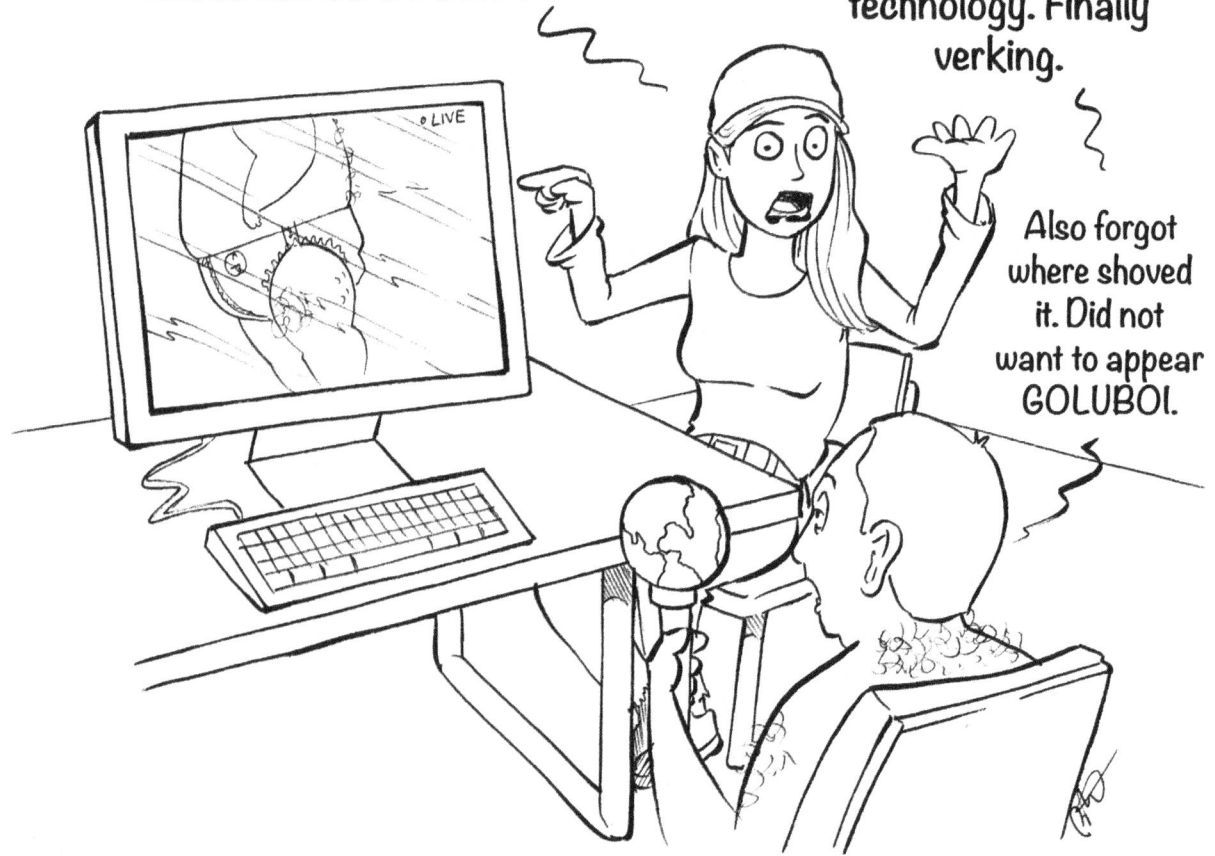

SOVIET STATE SECRET

THE RICH ARE "READ TO", SILLY HAND PUPPET!

A SERIES OF BURNING QUESTIONS

NOT JUST FOR HURRICANES

ACTIONS SPEAK LOUDER THAN WORDS

PULP FICTION WAS NEVER BIG IN RUSSIA

Our quest, little puppet friend, is at an end. So GOOD. Can't wait.

Welp. Guess I'm swapping out a greasy hand for a sticky hand... but at least I won't smell like chicken any more.

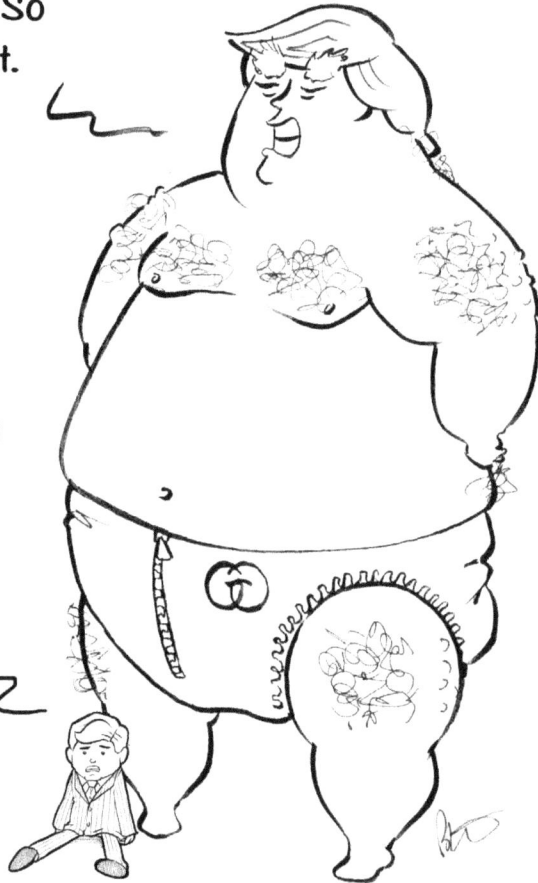

SEEING THE BRIGHT SIDE OF THINGS

I don't WANT to be the President of the World, any more. THIS is my so-good moment. THIS has been my one-and-only dream. I am young again. Soooo young, you don't even know.

SIMPLE GOALS = HAPPY LIFE

THE ROYAL TREATMENT

RAGE, RAGE AGAINST THE DYING OF THE LIGHT

ART IMITATES LIFE IMITATING LIFE

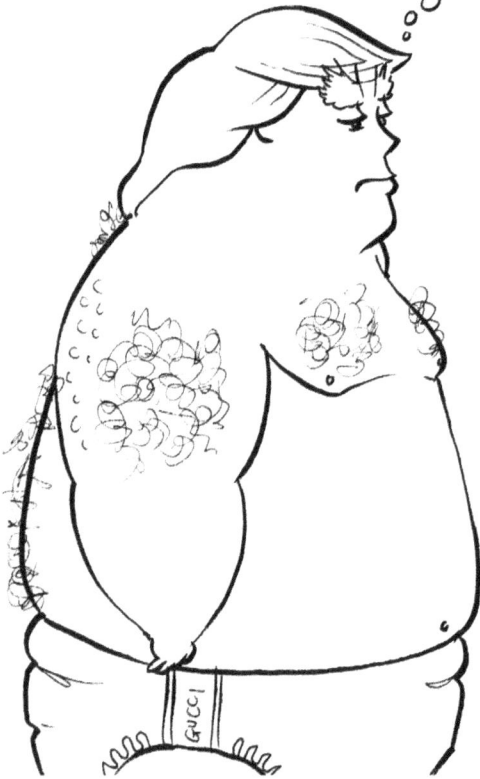

BESMIRCHED

THE WAYNE BRADY SYNDROME

WHAT LURKS IN THE SHADOWS

LIKE LOSING A NUCLEAR WARHEAD

PIRATE BOOTY

LIVE, LAUGH, LOVE

The excretion eminating from your EVACUATING pores reeks of FOWL in decay. This is UNCLEAN. If I am to touch you, but a tinge, in a manner outside of pure imagination, you mush wash TEN-FOLD followed by a drenching of White Gardenia Petals.

Only THEN may I partake in a solitary THOUGHT of approaching any closer than a centimeter.

What IS this STRANGE language?

WELL ABOVE HIS 3RD GRADE READING LEVEL

Get youself into a bath. You reek of a filthy East-Ender!

Proper attire is ESSENTIAL. Caravaning about in a soiled Gucci diaper is inadequate. I do NOT recognize Gucci as a brand of EXQUISITE quality!

Excessive body foliage is NOT permitted. This is why I didn't choose Harry.

I shant partake in vigorous intercourse with you until these conditions are met.

Yes, mother.

HIS MANHOOD DEFEATED, IF THERE EVER WAS SUCH A THING

"MUST LIKE DOGS"

NOT FOR ALL THE TEA IN CHIY-NAHH

Girls!!! I think we GOT HIM! His self-loving ego is fractured, his fictionally-measured manliness at near-zero. The end is within reach.. and how about MY ACCENT?! I love role-playing a bread-and-butter Brit. I AM BRITISH!!!

Talley-ho!! Pip-pip! Spot-o-tea. I can be PRIME MINISTER!!! We can DO this!

Who should I SCREW OVER next? The choices are as vast as the BRITISH EMPIRE!

THE HYPHENS WERE A DEAD GIVE-A-WAY

FORGET your blue balls, broken man-fantasies, and memories of unwanted maternal "exploration"... I just went face-to-face with the DEVIL DOG!!!

The Ghost of Roger Ailes CAN'T save me. Not anymore. Not ever!

ACTUALLY, NEVER COULD... BUT WHO'S COUNTING

A HILLARY-OUS "SOMETHING ABOUT MARY" MOMENT

EUNUCH IS NOT A CITY IN GERMANY

A COMMON MISCONCEPTION

THE BRITISH WAY

FOR THE GOOD OF SOCIETY

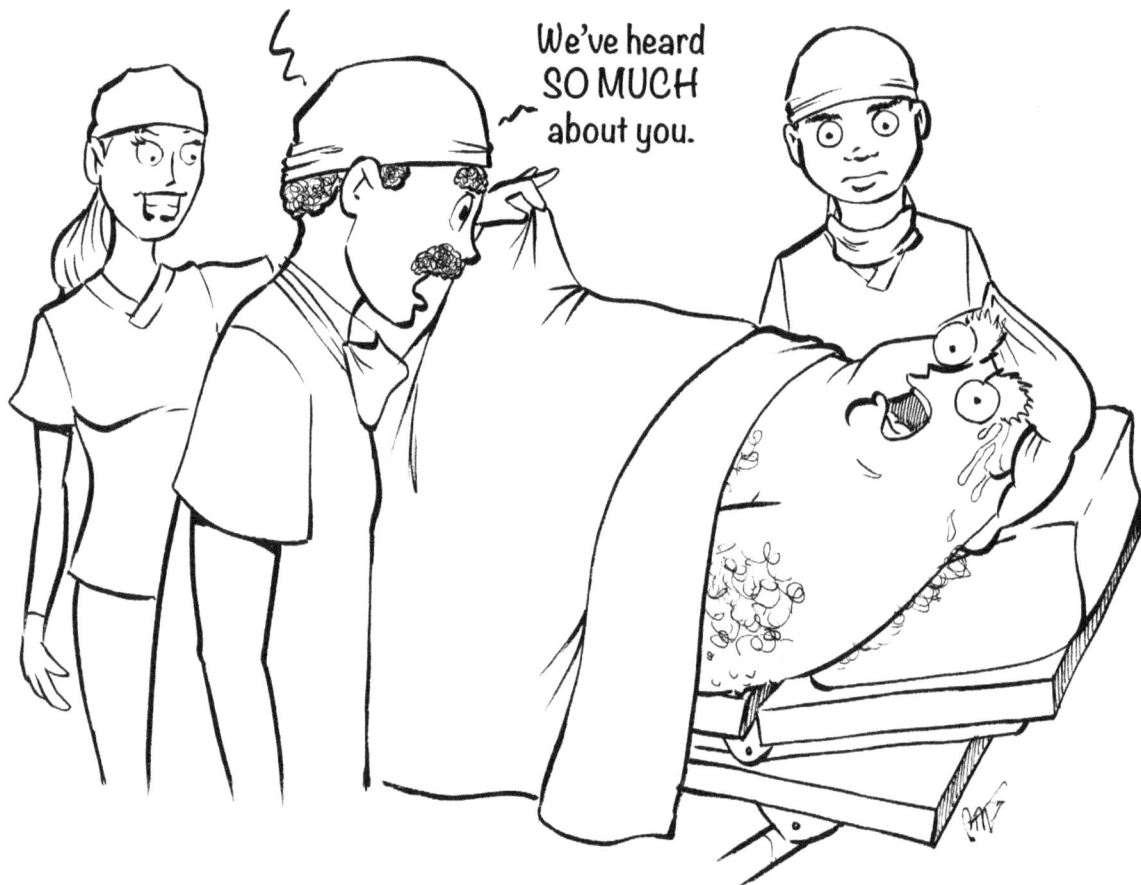

MEDICARE FOR ALL, AND TO ALL A GOOD NIGHT

BARBEQUES GALORE

TMZ EXCLUSIVE ALEC BALDWIN KNOCKING ON DEATH'S DOOR, RISKING HIS LIFE FOR METHOD

HE IS BECOMING

SO BRAVE

BETTER THAN BITCOIN

NOW 99% OF THE MAN HE USED TO BE

A NEW JOURNEY IS ABOUT TO BEGIN

Covfefe!! Where AM I? It's all a bunch of pure white empty space.... that's okay when it comes to people who vote for me, but THIS is completely different. BAD!!

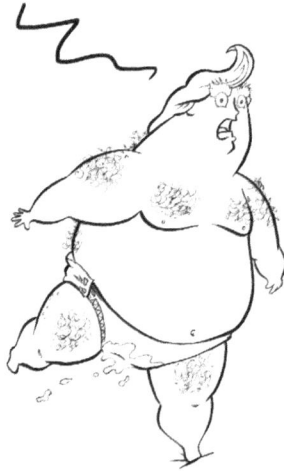

BE CAREFUL WHAT YOU WISH FOR

THE LIBERAL DEEP STATE IS...REAL????

No Da! No Vonka! No Fwens of Da he say there but nawt. E-Reek SAD an' ALONE. E-Reek told by Pooty he last one standing. What make E-Reek HAPPY?? Hunting cweatures with things that go BOOM make me happy.

E-Reek go to PORTLAND.

Hahaha. FUN for E-Reek.